Santa is coming to Scotland Colouring

CHILDHOOD DREAMS
HOMETOWN WORLD

Lost in the Snow

It was Christmas Eve, and a little robin was hurrying across Scotland. He was passing the post box when he spotted something lying in the snow. It was a letter addressed to Santa, but someone had dropped it and now all their Christmas wishes were lost. The little robin hopped down and picked it up in his beak. There was no time to lose!

3

Santa's Grotto

The little robin flapped his wings and set off for Santa's Grotto. He flew as fast as he could go. The letter in his beak felt heavier and heavier, but on and on the brave little robin flew.

Before long, the sky grew dark and the stars began to twinkle in the night sky. At last, the little robin could see the lights of Santa's Grotto glowing in the distance.

A letter for Santa

Santa was busy sorting out the last of the letters. Children from around the world had sent him their long wish lists. The little robin flew in and dropped the lost letter at Santa's feet.

"Hmmm, a mystery letter," said Santa, stroking his beard. "There is no address on this letter. However am I going to deliver these presents?"

Dear Santa
I have been very good this year, so I hope you are coming to my house on Christmas Eve.

I would like:
  a bike
  a DVD
  chocolate

Love
xxx

Santa's workshop

There was so much to do! Santa added the presents from the mystery letter to the Christmas list. Then he went into the workshop.

What a sight! There were elves busy tapping and fixing and painting and wrapping. As each parcel was labelled, Santa carefully ticked it off the list.

9

Flying away

Out in the crisp snow, the little robin watched as the elves helped Santa pack his sack into the sleigh. The reindeer stamped in the snow, while Santa made one last check to make sure he hadn't forgotten anything.

"Well, little robin," he said, "do you think you could help me find whoever sent the mystery letter?"

The little robin chirped. He would certainly try!

"Then, Scotland, here we come!" cried Santa as the sleigh climbed away into the frosty night sky.

The Big Apple

Santa and his sleigh flew on and on through the starry night. Far below, the lights of the towns and cities glowed.

"Ah, the Big Apple!" cried Santa as they dived in and out of the skyscrapers of New York City. The little robin took a break on top of the Statue of Liberty.

13

Flying over Paris

Before long, Santa's sleigh was whizzing over France. The lights of Paris shone brightly. The little robin stopped for a rest on top of the Eiffel Tower. It sparkled like a Christmas candle. From his perch, he could see Notre Dame and the Arc de Triomphe!

15

Dear old London Town

Soon, Santa could see the River Thames winding its way through London, criss-crossed with bridges.

BONG! BONG! BONG! BONG! BONG! BONG!

"Right on time," said Santa. "Big Ben is just striking midnight."

BONG! BONG! BONG! BONG! BONG! BONG!

17

Hello Scotland!

At last, Santa steered the sleigh towards Scotland. In the twinkling of an eye, they were flying above Loch Ness. The sleigh swooped high over Urquhart Castle and across the sparkling water. Is that Nessy?!

"I hope the cats and dogs are asleep this year!" laughed Santa. He patted his pocket. "But I have a special present for them in my pocket, just in case - choccy treats!"

19

Bonny Scotland

Santa lost no time delivering the presents. They flew from rooftop to rooftop all over Scotland. "On to the next house!" cried Santa as they flew off again.

The little robin flew over Bonny Scotland, following Santa's sleigh. They flew this way and that - from Inverness to Inverurie, from Perth to Paisley, from Ayr to Aberdeen - all over Scotland.

21

Rooftop landing

In no time at all, Santa was delivering the last of the presents. The reindeer landed lightly on the rooftop and the sleigh slid to a stop. Santa stepped out and lifted his sack over his shoulder.

"This is our last stop, little robin," said Santa, "unless we can find our mystery letter sender!"

23

An empty stocking

The little robin was tired out. As he rested, he spotted a light on in a window. The little robin hopped onto the window ledge and peeped in.

In bed was a child fast asleep. At the bottom of the bed was an empty stocking. Why hadn't Santa filled the stocking? wondered the little robin. It must be the mystery letter sender! The little robin flew off at once to tell Santa.

A bit of a squeeze!

The little robin found Santa just as he was packing up his sack. When he heard about the empty stocking, Santa jumped back in the sleigh and followed the little robin back to the house with the light in the window.

Clutching his sack, Santa stepped carefully into the chimneypot and disappeared.

27

under the Christmas tree

Santa put the big parcels under the Christmas tree. Someone had left a plate with a mince pie and a glass of milk. Santa nibbled the pie and sipped the milk.

"Just right!" said Santa, patting his tummy. Then, he crept quietly upstairs to fill up the stocking at the end of the bed with small Christmas surprises.

Merry Christmas!

The little robin and the reindeer waited patiently until Santa popped out of the chimney again with his empty sack and climbed back into the sleigh.

"Well done, little robin," chuckled Santa. "You've saved Christmas Day!"

As the stars twinkled brightly above, the reindeer scampered off the roof pulling Santa and his sleigh behind them.

"Merry Christmas, Scotland!"

31

Have you written a letter to Santa? Remember to write your address. And don't drop it!

Written by Katherine Sully
Illustrated by Simon Abbott
Designed by Sarah Allen

First published by HOMETOWN WORLD in 2013
Hometown World Ltd
7 Northumberland Buildings
Bath BA1 2JB

www.hometownworld.co.uk

ISBN 978-1-84993-593-7
Printed in China